Eerie Planet
Second Edition

*A Photographic Exploration
of Dark Tourism*

Marquis H.K.

©**Serial Pleasures**, 2023
www.serialpleasures.com

ISBN: 979-8-86802-542-6

Table of contents

Introduction

I initially began the follow up to *Eerie Planet* in 2019 , for various reasons it took way longer than expected. The most obvious of course being the global pandemic which instated a worldwide travel ban. Most of the places featured within these pages I did manage to get to before the dreaded covid put the whole world into lockdown. One of which – Chernobyl, proved rather fortunate with the timing as I was lucky enough to travel there before the war in Ukraine. I spent two years in the Channel Islands researching and photographing some of the location contained herein. Some locations have been revisited from the first edition of this book . The reason for this is that I felt these places required more in -depth further exploration. As I feel in the first edition I just scratched the surface.

Overall a lot more work as gone into this edition. The main feature being more full colour photographs. I certainly enjoyed putting it together. Seeking out and exploring these places gives me gratification to no end. It gives me great pleasure to share these experiences with you.

The Author

Acknowledgements

The following people are owed my gratitude for contributing to this project in one way or another.

Paul ' Stoney' Stone – OTP Graphics for front , back cover and spine design . Nico Claux – Serial Pleasures, Simon Gilberthorpe, Andy Jones – Littledean Jail/Crime Through Time Museum, J A Henderson, James Corstorphine – City of the Dead Tours, Paul Bourgaize – Festung Guernsey, Mike Bell – Loch Ness Cruises, Lance Gilbert, Mark Pontin – Bel Air Inn – Isle of Sark, Taxi Tommy Car Service – Huntington – West Virginia , Bill's Taxis – Alderney, Martyn Blondel Taxi – Guernsey. Steve Windle – Ripon Taxis.

Caynton Caves

Located just outside the UK village of Shifnal in the county of Shropshire is a series of underground man made chambers and caverns known as the Caynton Caves. They are hollowed out of sandstone and consist of carved archways, pillars and niches for candles. There are also ancient looking carvings on the stone.

They are located in deep woodland in a disused quarry on the grounds of Caynton Hall. The caves entrance is literally at the foot of a tree like a rabbit hole. They are on private grounds and not open to the public. So visiting there is essentially trespassing although so many youtubers, paranormal investigators and bloggers disregard this fact.

The caves true purpose is unknown, there are speculations that they date back to the 17th century. Another theory is that they may have even been associated with the Knights Templar. Although the Templars were dissolved in the 14th century so this is highly unlikely. However In the late 1980's an authentic medieval sword was recovered from the caverns. Local resident Mark Lawnton who found it had it evaluated and it turns out it dates back to the 13th century possibly belonging to a member of the Knights Templar.

During the 1980's they were used for informal meetings, ceremonies and black magic rituals for numerous occult groups.

Of course when I first learned of these it was like a red rag to a bull for me . I just had to check them out for myself. It took two visits to find them, the first visit I was in the wrong location on the other side of the Caynton Hall property. I even tried ringing the bell asking for permission to visit, but the voice on the intercom advised me that what I was looking for wasn't on their property. So I gave it up as a bad job and caught the pre-booked cab back to my B&B in the nearby town of Telford.

However a good friend of mine – Mr Simon Gilberthorpe sent me a google earth image pinpointing the exact location of the caves in the woods. This time I knew where to go, so within two weeks I was back. It's around a twenty minute drive from Telford, it's in the middle of nowhere so of course there is no public transport. In my case I had to catch a cab there and back.

Once there one has to jump the fence and walk along a barbed wire fence on the perimeter of the woods. As with the case with the Abbey of Thelema someone had cut a hole in the fence with wire cutters. I knew for sure then that I was in the right location. I made my way down a steep ditch and through the woodland. It was January so it was cold and damp, and there I saw it , through the trees, the rabbit hole entrance. I brought a strong flashlight with me as it would have been pitch dark in there and getting photos without one would've been near impossible. However I needn't have bothered. There were three other people there already who had lit the whole interior of the caverns up with tea lights. It looked pretty darned spectacular, they were world explorer professional photographers and had their tripods set up.

I just let them do their own thing whilst I did my own exploring. They were friendly enough, even somewhat concerned about a cut on my face that I sustained whilst getting over the fence from a thorn branch!

The place was everything I expected and more , totally amazing. An hidden underground labyrinth. It reminded me of an ancient temple excavation from an *Exorcist* movie . You can see why this place attracted occult and black magic groups. It's the perfect location for a ceremonial gathering. I explored for an hour or so before heading back to the rendezvous spot for my cab. Whilst waiting I downed a couple of lagers to celebrate, mission accomplished.

The rabbit hole Caynton Cave entrance at the foot of the tree.

The hidden underground labyrinth.

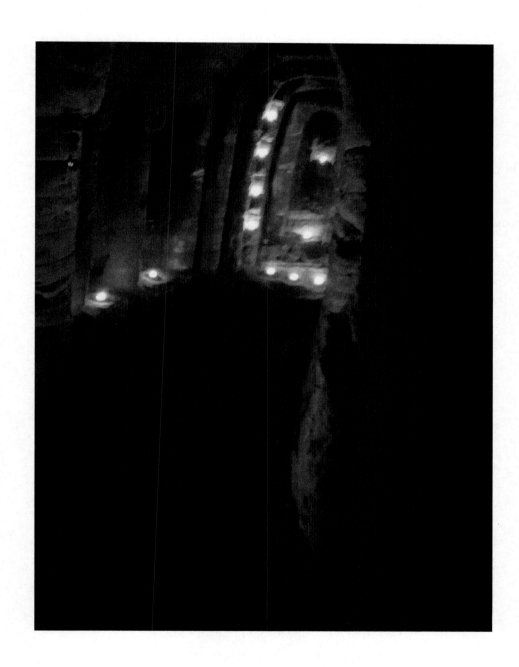

Druid's Temple

Located in North Yorkshire just outside the market town of Masham is the Druid's Temple. And though it certainly looks ancient and authentic it is in fact less than 200 years old. It was built in the 19th century as a folly styled after stone circle monuments such as Stonehenge. The construction was also an incentive to alleviate local unemployment at the time.

I've visited the temple on two occasions. The most recent was on Halloween 2020 . It is located in a secluded woodland and is very atmospheric. It would be the perfect location to shoot a scene for a horror movie or a music clip.

There is no public transport that goes nere there so you have to drive to the entrance. From there you make your way up a path which leads to the path in the woodland and the temple is a short walk from there. I caught a taxi from the town of Ripon on both occasions but it was well worth it. It is well hidden so if you chose to hold a ritual or ceremony there it's a pretty safe bet you wouldn't be disturbed. It is indeed the perfect spot for a ceremonial occult gathering. There wasn't a soul around when I visited on both occasions. It's definitely worth a visit if you're into creepy looking atmospheric places. Being in a wooded area it also has an eerie silence about it.

It is comprised of rows of circular standing stones and in the centre is a flat stone which resembles a sacrificial altar in front of a dark cave.

Halloween revelry at the temple.

UK industrial hardcore band Juratory used the temple as the location
for a photoshoot . Photo courtesy of Paul 'Stoney' Stone.

Littledean Jail - Crime Through Time Collection

Located just outside the city pf Gloucester at the entrance to the Forest of Dean in south west England lies an 18th century former prison. Built in 1788 it served as a House of Corrections for the likes of petty thieves, prostitutes, fraudsters and offenders guilty of violent and anti-social behaviour. In 1854 it became redundant as a prison and served as a police station until 1972. It also served as a petty sessional court until 1985. Today it serves a similar purpose but houses not inmates but something equally controversial and notorious – the U.K.'s most infamous and politically incorrect 'black museum'.

Owner Andy Jones and his family purchased the jail partly as a family home and to house his 'Crime Through Time Collection'.

The whole building is packed from floor to ceiling with macabre and infamous collectibles. Everything from serial killer murderabillia, authentic Nazi items, celebrity sleaze, political scandal, occult satanism and witchcraft, items owned by infamous gangsters and violent criminals, secret societies, pop and punk culture and much, much more.

I'd first seen Littledean Jail on the Netflix series *Dark Tourist* and it really struck a chord with me. I just had to visit this place! So in 2019 I did just that. I got in contact with Andy and explained that I wanted to include the jail in the 2nd edition of *Eerie Planet*. He liked the idea , we arranged to meet and he opened up the jail for me.

Andy describes his exhibition as '*Where Good and Evil Collide*' as it consists as heroes such as James Bond, Batman, Bruce Lee, The Punisher and the British SAS. As well as evil villains fact and fiction. He is a stone mason by trade and describes his exhibition as a '*hobby gone wrong*'.

From the minute I entered I was gobsmacked, I've seen some collections but never anything like this. I've been a collector myself most of my life but this was a serious lifetime commitment. It certainly put any collector stores I've been to shame. I could've literally spent days here not hours. Though I have to say this exhibition certainly isn't for the faint of heart. There are more than a few items that are guaranteed to offend some individuals. It is not a family friendly museum. However it is a true crime and pop culture enthusiasts paradise. Of course this has also come with more than it's fair share of flack. Andy has been subjected to protests, obscenity prosecutions and threats of boycott. But he has stood his ground for over two decades. This is a historically significant, no holds barred museum. Don't like it, don't come. Simple.

Some of the signage outside the museum warning
against those easily offended not to enter.

WARNING

LITTLEDEAN JAIL
UNLOCKED

CRIME
THROUGH
TIME

THE BLACK MUSEUM

Above – pagan Wiccan temple designed by museum owner Andy.

I arrived at the jail on a Tuesday afternoon (a day that it's not open). I met Andy out the front we chatted for a while and he proceeded to give me the grand tour. We had a lot in common, not just our shared interest of the museum's contents but we are both old punk rockers. He used to play in a band called Demob who I remember from the first Punk and Disorderly compilation LP released in 1982.

I began the tour with the occult and witchcraft exhibit. There was lots of cool devil's heads, ritual tools, statues, inverted pentagrams and some information display boards on Aleister Crowley.

Next was the '*Where Good and Evil Collide*' exhibit. I recognised this from the Netflix *Dark Tourist* episode. But it was another thing being here in person. There was just so much to see and take in, not an ounce of free space. Not just horror movie icons, but original items from the initial punk explosion. Notably the Johnny Rotten long sleeved cheesecloth 'Destroy' shirt. A pair of Sid Vicious's motorcycle boots are also on display. As well as lifesize figures of the Russian mad monk Rasputin. This place is... incredible.

The next section is a history of fascism, this includes the Nazi Holocaust and Third Reich, fascist Britain and the Ku Klux Klan. Now there are some items and displays in this section that are sure to cause offence to some. Genuine SS uniforms and instruments of torture from death camps. Mannequins dressed in KKK hoods posing with gollywog dolls. But perhaps the most disturbing thing is a diorama depicting brutality and rape in a concentration camp. Even I thought this was a bit too much. But as Andy says, this happened and we can't ignore it.

Next up was the true crime section featuring items that belonged to some of the most notorious criminals in recent history. There were knuckledusters belonging to infamous London gangsters the Kray Twins, one of Ronnie Kray's suits, tracksuits worn by UK celebrity criminal Charles Bronson (a good mate of Andy's) and disgraced UK TV /radio personality Jimmy Saville. Graphic depictions of atrocities committed by ISIS adorned one wall and of course a section devoted to serial killers. They were all there – John Wayne Gacy, Charles Manson, David Berkowitz, Ed Gein, Moors Murderers Ian Brady and Myra Hindley, Yorkshire Ripper Peter Sutcliffe, Jeffrey Dahmer and The Night Stalker Richard Ramirez – someone who I also wrote to for ten years as chronicled in my 2020 book *Letters From The Night Stalker – A Decade's Correspondence With Richard Ramirez -*   Fully illustrated display boards adorned with photos, newspaper clippings, autographed photos, artwork and letters.

Indeed one of the UK's most horrific murder cases in history occurred literally in Andy's backyard. Fred and Rosemary West murdered 12 young women between 1967 – 1987. Their victims were subjected to rape, torture bondage and mutilation to satisfy their sick sexual gratification. The dismembered bodies were

found buried in the cellar and under the patio in the garden of 25 Cromwell Street, Gloucester. What came to be known as the 'House of Horrors'.

Many items from the House of Horrors are on display in this museum. Including Fred and Rose West's clothing, furniture, gardening tools (including the shovel used to bury the victims) and even the prison bench which Fred West slept on when he was first arrested. Of course I did ask Andy how he comes into possession of such macabre artifacts. He has an inner circle of contacts including friends in the police force. A relationship which he says is all based upon trust. I wasn't about to probe any further.

I made my way through the walls of celebrity sleaze and scandal. There was a framed signed pair of white silky panties mounted on a collage of tabloid articles of the owner.

Then there was a wall of impressive oil painting portraits of just about every notorious figure in history you could think of. All beautifully painted with a reference to their history beside their image. This was something else. There were also monitors playing a documentary on the Church of Satan. As previously stated, I could have spent days here.

Original authentic Sex Pistols posters.

Signed poster of *The Shining*.

Oil painting portraits of infamous figures in history
depicted on the Littledean Jail flyer – from the
author's collection .

Autographed photos and movie stills from *Quadrophenia*.

Finally it was on to an exhibit of what's regarded as the best youth culture film of all time, and one of my personal favourites – *Quadrophenia*. Released in 1979 and set in 1960's London, it tells the story of bitter rival youth gangs, the mods and the rockers. With Phil Daniels as Jimmy the mod, the angst ridden, pill popping protagonist and Brighton Beach being the designated battlefield and war zone. The film has a massive cult following worldwide.

The exhibit consisted of lots of signed photos from the stars – Phil Daniels, Mark Wingett, Leslie Ash, Phil Davis and Ray Winstone.

There was also movie stills, original posters, clothing from the film's wardrobe and Lambretta scooters belonging to Jimmy and Ace Face (Sting) used in the movie.

James Bond 007 collection and life size Dalek
featured in the '*Where Good and Evil Collide*' exhibit.

It was time to head back to my hotel in Gloucester. I was leaving the following day and there was things I had to organise before my departure. Andy offered to give me a lift to my hotel but there was one more thing he had to show me. On the way there he was telling me some funny stories of the drunken shenhanigans he got up to with the *Dark Tourist* crew along with Charles Bronson's then wife and former actress Paula Williamson (now sadly deceased). Turns out it took five days to film that one segment.

Alas we arrived at our destination, where it all happened, the crimes that shook the world – Cromwell Street. The *'House of Horrors'* was demolished in 1996, two years after the Wests' were arrested. It is now a public walkway with bollards linking the adjacent street. The locals understandably want to put that part of history well and truly behind them. Apparently they don't take too kindly to thrill seeking dark tourists. Andy drove slowly up and down the street trying to provoke a reaction but there was none.

Littledean Jail can easily be accessed by public transport. You just catch a number 22 bus from the Gloucester transport hub and it is a thirty minute journey. An absolute must if you're into all this stuff. Though it is only open from Thursday – Sundays and Monday bank holidays.

Above – The spot where Fred and Rose West's *'House of Horrors'* on
25 Cromwell Street once stood.

The author Marquis and Littledean Jail owner Andy.

Edinburgh Vaults / Greyfriar's Graveyard

Hidden within the nineteen arches of Edinburgh's South Bridge is a series of chambers ranging in size known as the Edinburgh Vaults. They were constructed in 1788 and used to house taverns, workshops and storage space for these business'. However due to lack of sunlight , dampness and poor air quality, conditions in the vaults deteriorated.

It soon became a hotspot for the homeless and a slum for the city's poor population. It was seen as a solution to put the poor underground in a subterranean city to manage overpopulation. Living conditions were appalling with no running water or sanitation and the only light provided by fish oil lamps.

This in turn also caused criminal activity to flourish. It became the city's red light district with multiple brothels, illegal gambling and whisky distillery. Robbery and murder also plagued the vaults and there are even stories of bodysnatchers storing corpses there.

The vaults were eventually closed off for good in 1875. They were rediscovered in the 1980's and excavated in the 1990's. Hundreds of tonnes of rubble was removed that had been dumped in there. Edinburgh ghost tour company City of the Dead now operate nightly tours there. It is regarded as one of the most haunted locations on the planet .

Edinburgh is also home to the Greyfriar's Graveyard which allegedly houses a very real angry poltergeist. Within the Greyfriar's grounds is the former Covenanter's Prison. It is here where some 1,200 Presbyterian Covenanters were imprisoned after their defeat by the Scottish Government at the Battle of Bothwell Bridge in 1679. Some were executed whilst others died of maltreatment. The person responsible for this was George 'Bloody' MacKenzie. He has a tomb in the form of a mausoleum within the grounds and it is his poltergeist that has been known to physically attack visitors.

People visiting the site have reported unexplained cuts, bruises, red welts and even physically knocked to the ground. It is known as the 'Black Mausoleum'.

City of the Dead Tours have exclusive access to the Covenanter's Prison. They offer a 'Double Dead' tour which includes a complete tour of the vaults and the prison. I went on one of these tours on a cold January night in 2020. I'm happy to say I came out unscathed with the exception of what I suspected was a mandatory jump scare from another tour guide. Unfortunately I can't say the same for my photography. Most of the photos I took were way too dark to use in this book. As a result most appear courtesy of City of the Dead which are credited. Both locations are genuinely creepy and the tour's reviews and awards are absolutely merited.

Edinburgh Vaults

Photos courtesy of City of the Dead Tours.

Photos courtesy of City of the Dead Tours .

I spoke with author and City of the Dead Tours founder J A Henderson on how he started the company and his take on the MacKenzie Poltergeist.

How did City of the Dead tours come about and what made you start it up?

I got talking to a caretaker at Greyfriars Graveyard, who began telling me about a mysterious entity that had recently begun attacking people in Greyfriars. I was already working for an Edinburgh tour company and figured this was a chance to strike out on my own. I called the entity the 'Mackenzie Poltergeist' and started tours to investigate what was going on. I had no idea just how spectacularly it would take off or how famous the poltergeist would become. It's now the best documented supernatural case of all time.

Have you ever had any experiences firsthand with the Mackenzie Poltergeist or seen anyone physically attacked by it? Or any other paranormal activity you care to elaborate on?

The Mackenzie Poltergeist is something you feel more than see, though he seems to leave the guides alone. Well... mostly. But I've seen plenty. Take the five children who began screaming in unison that something was choking them. I thought they'd cooked up the story together (which would have been an awesome prank) until I realised none of them knew each other. Or the minister who tried to exorcise the poltergeist. He told myself and a reporter he had never experienced anything like it and feared the fight might kill him - then died a few weeks later. Or the loud American who rubbished everything I was saying before toppling, out cold, into a large puddle. I quite liked Mackenzie for that.

Of course, it could all be psychosomatic, but the sheer volume of evidence is overwhelming, and I'm not inclined to call thousands of eyewitnesses liars. I have many photographs of injuries inflicted by the poltergeist and over 100 pages of eyewitness accounts emailed to me. I've counted dozens of birds, lying unmarked but dead, inside the Prison. On every tour a visitor will complain that their camera phone or watch has stopped working. I've seen the aftermath of numerous fires that break out around Greyfriars - including the one that burned my house in the graveyard to the ground..

You now reside in Australia , what made you move to the other side of the world and run the tours from there? Is it just as easy to run there as it is in Edinburgh?

In this technologically advance world it's fairly easy to run anything from anywhere. In fact, I'm sure some of the staff haven't noticed I'm gone. It would be good for business to say the Poltergeist scared me away (and my business partner emigrated to New Zealand!). Truth is, however, I wanted an adventure. And to see some actual sun.

But perhaps the most peculiar thing with all of this is when I approached Jan for an interview. He replied with an email stating he couldn't talk with me in person as he now resided in Australia. I'd just moved to the UK from Australia at the time so I asked him where he was living. Now , as big as Australia is , it turns out he was living just off my old street in my suburb in Brisbane!

Image courtesy of City of the Dead Tours.

Shadowy creepy figures. City of the Dead Tours official logo.
Image courtesy of City of the Dead Tours.

Loch Ness

Another location I covered in the first edition of this book however I feel Loch Ness definitely warrants another visit. Since writing the first book I have returned here on several occasions and at the time of writing this I am currently based and working here at Nessieland Exhibition and Gift Shop.

I can certainly say that interest in the loch and what may inhabit it is as strong as ever. I get asked constantly if I've seen the legendary beast which I haven't as yet but I have spoken with people who have seen something. Of course there are still many theories of what it may be and the sightings continue. The most common concept being a long necked humped leviathan creature. Although sightings have varied in description throughout the years. Many reports of sightings come from respectable members of the community who would have absolutely nothing to gain by concocting a story. My local barber in Inverness knows a resident in the village of Foyers who claims the residents there always knew that something inhabited the loch but kept it to themselves. For the simple reason they didn't want a media frenzy spoiling the tranquil village. However science as yet to prove a valid existence. And as the sightings continue so do the hoaxes and fakers.

Nessie hunter Steve Feltham is still camped on Dores Beach where he has been for the last thirty two years only to see what he calls possibilities.

In his book *Nessie – Exploring the Supernatural Origins of the Loch Ness Monster*, author Nick Redfern explores the theory that Nessie may be something completely different to what we're led to believe. A supernatural phenomena rather than a flesh- and- blood creature. This would certainly explain how it is seen yet evades capture and remains undetected. He also examines ghostly spectres that haunt the loch and evidence linking it with the occult. Including dragon worshipping cults and of course the possible conjuring of something from occultist Aleister Crowley who inhabited Boleskine House on the shores of the loch from 1899-1913 for the sole purpose of performing the Abramelin Operation ritual.

The whole history of the loch is steeped in legend, folklore and mythology. It certainly has an atmosphere of intrigue and mystery. It lies on the Great Glen Fault Line and was formed by glacier erosion around 10,000 years ago. The deepest part is in the vicinity of Urquhart Castle nearing 800 feet. A few feet from the shoreline it plunges to a sheer drop. It has exceptionally low visibility below the surface due to the high peat content in the surrounding soil, a black abyss.

On a clear sunny day the loch can look picturesque and tranquil with the blue sky reflecting off the surface. On a cold overcast day it can look downright sinister. Uninviting and foreboding.

Mike Bell has been the skipper of the Nessie Hunter boat for the last 4.5 years and hosts daily cruises. He took over from renowned Nessie seeker George Edwards who is now retired. He's experienced deep diving in the loch first hand. I sat down with him on a pleasant afternoon on Temple Pier to get his take on things.

'There is light for ten metres below the surface, beyond that no sunlight gets through. You can't see your hand in front of you, no vegetation grows down there. The temperature is five degrees and doesn't change. As far as what may reside in there I don't have an opinion because I don't know and I don't think anyone knows. I'll say that as a person that spends every day on the loch any theory is plausible. Because with all the modern technology such as sophisticated sonar we haven't even scratched the surface. Operation Deepscan did pick up sonar contacts around 4-5 metres but they could have just been floating logs. It's hard to know because we know so little about the loch and it's ecology. As far as earthquakes, wind funnels and other natural phenomena that it's hard to understand what we can't study. We do have fun with the whole myth thing though. We've built props for kids charities and the joy it can bring to people is unbelievable.'

Mike Bell and his boat Nessie Hunter.

Of course the hardened skeptics will always argue that the sightings are nothing more than other animals such as birds, swimming deer or the occasional seals, boat wake or floating driftwood.

Scientists have also theorised that it could be what's known as a seiche. This is when strong winds and rapid air pressure pushes the water from one side of the loch to the other. This is a back and forth effect that creates turbulence. This can dislodge logs and other debris stuck at the bottom of the loch and bring it to the surface. Which in turn get mistaken for sightings. It could also be natural phenomenon created due to a long term effect of the Great Glen Fault. Upward waves and ripples arising from seismic activity. Creating the impression of a large animal moving below the surface.

Whatever the case may be, even if irrefutable evidence was presented to them in the form of a crystal clear up close photo, in this age of photoshop and artificial intelligence, skeptics would simply dismiss it as someone's clever creation.

Folklore states that the creature inhabiting the loch could be what is known in Scottish mythology as a 'Kelpie' or water-horse. These were malevolent shape-shifting creatures who devoured their prey and dragged them into the depths. This tale dates back to the 6th century Irish monk St Columba who legend has it banished a beast from the River Ness which was about to attack a man swimming in the river. This story was handed down through generations as an old wives tale which was used to warn children to stay away from the deep, murky waters of the loch.

Though the most common concept of Nessie is that of a colony of plesiosaurs that somehow survived the ice age and became trapped in the loch. They were reptilian creatures with four flippers, long neck and small head which grew to around fifteen feet in length. However they have been extinct for over sixty five million years, they also dwelt in shallow salt waters and breathed air. So if this was the case and the loch was somehow inhabited by a bunch of plesiosaurs it would be seen on an almost daily basis. And the fact that the loch is fresh water, too cold for reptiles and around ten thousand years old makes this theory scientifically impossible.

This theory was of course fuelled by the iconic 1934 'surgeon's photo'. Which depicted a plesiosaur creature with its long neck and small head protruding out of the water. This enigma was put to bed forever in 1994 when one Christian Spurling made a deathbed confession that he had assisted in creating a model using plastic and wood materials and attaching them to a toy submarine.

The photo was also cropped giving the impression that the 'creature' was bigger than it actually was. When you see the whole photo it's literally around the size of a duck!

However in May 1977 another sighting of a plesiosaur – like creature was photographed. This time in full colour by Anthony 'Doc' Shiels. It depicted a long serpentine neck with a small head protruding around five feet out of the water. It was of a green brownish colour with a pale yellowish front. It created such an uproar that it made front page of the Daily Mirror – one of the UK's biggest selling newspapers. My old man read the Mirror on a daily basis, I was nine years old at the time and remember it well. The headline screamed '*UP FOR THE JUBILEE NESSIE!*' (1977 was the year of the Queen's silver jubilee).

Shiels was a skilled magician and wizard and claimed that he used magic to conjure the beast. Of course being a magician meant that he was also an expert trickster and even on more than one occasion explained how to carry out a convincing hoax. Of course this has made his detractors more than a little dubious over the years. However to this day he remains adamant that the photo that he took at Loch Ness is the real deal . And it has never been disproven.

Likewise with the Hugh Gray photo from November 1933. It was the first official Nessie photo to be published and shows what appears to be an animal with a flipper or tail on the surface of the loch. The image is quite blurred and appears to show the spraying of water. Some skeptics came to the conclusion that it was nothing more than an out of focus photo of a Labrador dog retrieving a stick in it's mouth. Detailed analysis however proved that this certainly was not the case. Then there was the Peter MacNab photo from July 27th 1955. It was taken at Urquhart Castle and depicts a huge object with two humps in the water moving towards the castle. The castle tower is forty feet tall so judging from the photo this is estimated to be around sixty feet in length. Again it has never been disproven.

The early 70's saw some iconic underwater shots of what appeared to be a flipper and a full body shot of a creature with a long neck taken by research scientist Dr Robert Rines. Resident Loch Ness skeptic Adrian Shine is fully vocal that these images were retouched and manipulated before finding their way to magazine publishers.

These are just some examples of some of the iconic photos taken throughout the years. There have of course been many more but it would be something of a futile exercise to scrutinise every photo for a tourism themed photographic book such as this.

The first video footage of the creature was taken in 1960 by cryptozoologist Tim Dinsdale. It is a black and white film and shows the creature swimming in a circular formation before submerging and creating a V-shaped wake. This led to the formation of the Loch Ness Investigation Bureau. Something they decided was definitely out there.

Of course there is also the phenomenon known as pareidolia – that which the human eye attempts to interpret random imagery for something much more than what it actually is. We've seen this used at disaster sites when what appears to be a demonic face in the cloud of smoke. A scientific term for seeing what one wants to see.

Urquhart Castle seen from the Nessie Hunter. The focal point of Loch Ness and hotspot for Nessie sightings. It has also seen it's share of bloodshed and upheaval throughout it's history, including the Jacobite Rebellion.

The shores at Urquhart Castle. It's only a narrow space beyond the shore
before a sudden plunge into the abyss.

On a clear sunny day the loch can give the impression
of a beautiful tranquil stretch of water.

Of course there is the question that if large creatures did inhabit the loch for all these years then why hasn't any remains or carcasses ever been found? This is because whatever dies in the loch tends to stay there. The cold dark waters prevent decomposition and gases which causes the body to bloat and rise to the surface. So whatever dies in there the loch claims as it's own forever. Though a World War ll Wellington Bomber that crash landed in the loch was recovered in 1985. It was surprisingly well preserved considering it had been sitting at the bottom of the loch for nearly forty-five years. The navigation lights even still worked when connected to a modern battery. It now resides in Brooklands Aviation Museum in the UK. Though a Nessie movie prop which sank during the filming of the 1973 film *The Private Life of Sherlock Holmes* still sits exactly where it sank to this very day.

The author at the iconic Urquhart Castle.

Though Urquhart Castle is the focal point of Loch Ness and the hotspot for Nessie sightings it is also the busiest, especially during peak season. There are bus loads of tourists turning up every day. If you don't book in advance online chances are you won't get in. There is also a fifteen pound admission fee. However there are other parts of the loch that offer magnificent views that you can enjoy free off charge with minimum crowds.

Heading towards Inverness on the A82 is the Clansman Hotel. It is the only hotel located on the banks of the loch and has a restaurant with magnificent panoramic views overlooking the loch. I've frequented there a few times and it is a great place to have a pint whilst searching for Nessie. There is also a life size plesiosaur out the front for photo opportunities. The shores of the loch can be accessed by a road underpass which brings you out on to the marina where they run hourly boat cruises.

It is also here that the former Clansman owner had a monster encounter. Catherine Handley was walking through the car park around 6pm when she heard a loud splashing coming from the marina. She described it as something huge thrashing around in the water like it was trapped struggling to get free. She didn't investigate what it was. She was so scared she ran with her daughter to their on site flat and locked the door. She went and had a look the next day but of course whatever had been there was long gone.

Located virtually opposite on the other side of the loch is the Dores Inn Pub. It features what is my favourite beer garden on Dores Beach right on the loch shores. It has a tiny bar in the beer garden itself with a Nessie styled archway . It is a fantastic place to spend an afternoon with a few pints gazing down the loch.

It is here where Nessie hunter Steve Feltham is camped in his van. He has been here for the last thirty two years searching for Nessie and continues to do so on a daily basis. He has also become the go to guy for the media whenever they're covering a story on the monster.

View from the Clansman Restaurant overlooking the loch.

Life size plesiosaur out the front of the Clansman.

The Clansman Marina where daily boat cruises operate. It is here where the former hotel owner had an encounter with the monster when she heard something big thrashing around in the water.

Dores Inn Beer Garden. A fantastic place to
enjoy a beer overlooking the loch.

Nessie hunter Steve Feltham with his van
on Dores Beach where he's been for the last
thirty two years searching for Nessie.

Foyers is a split level village divided between upper and lower. The lower part is on the shores of the loch itself and hosts an awesome little campsite – The Loch Ness Shores campsite. It is located right on the banks of the loch in a secluded quiet location. There is no traffic or busy roads nearby . An ideal tranquil place tom take in the loch's mystery. There is facilities and mini cabins on site. At the time of writing I have a cabin booked for Halloween 2023. Upper Foyers is a steep climb through a forest walking trail. It hosts the Falls of Foyers, a spectacular waterfall with a hundred and forty foot drop into a gorge which winds it's way through trees and down into the loch. The village also hosts a tea room and general store. The 302 bus route takes you straight here and also goes by the aforementioned Dores Beach and past Boleskine House and cemetery.

Another location to visit in Inverness is the Culloden Battlefield. It is the site of the last pitched battle to be fought on British soil on April 16 1746. The bloody battle only lasted an hour and put an end to the Jacobite uprising led by Bonnie Prince Charlie. His weary army were defeated by government forces led by the Duke of Cumberland. After which Prince Charlie was forced to go into exile. It is located around twenty minutes outside Inverness and features an informative visitor centre and guided tours of the site.

Just up the road from Culloden Battlefield are the ancient Clava Cairns Burial Chambers. They are around 4,000 years old and were built during the Bronze Age. The site consists of three burial chambers and standing stones. In winter the setting sun aligns with the stones and is on all accounts a magical sight. The site is open to the public and there is no admission fee. However no public transport goes there. The closest bus stop is Culloden and is not exactly walking distance. The best thing to do is do as I did and work out a deal with a cab driver whereupon he drops and waits whilst you explore.

Cabins on the Loch Ness Shores campsite
overlooking the loch in Lower Foyers.

The shores of the loch adjacent to the
campsite grounds.

Clan memorial stone on Culloden Battlefield.

Clava Cairns ancient burial chambers and standing stones.

Boleskine House Revisited

Another location I covered in the first edition of this book but again that deserves another visit here is Boleskine House. The main reason being that the house has literally been risen from the dead. First a bit of history for those not in the know. It is located on the south east side of Loch Ness near the tranquil village of Foyers. It's most famous or infamous resident is occultist Aleister Crowley who resided there from 1899 – 1913.

Crowley purchased the property for one specific purpose. To perform a ritual known as the Sacred Magic of Abramelin the Mage. For this he required a house of complete seclusion. The purpose of the ritual is to invoke one's guardian angel. But it also involves summoning the 12 kings and dukes of hell to bind them and remove their negative influences from the magicians life.

However Crowley was summoned to Paris and never completed the ritual, thus never banishing the demons from the house. This led to some strange goings on and sinister occurrences at the house. Including future residents going mad and one blowing his head off with a shotgun in Crowley's former bedroom. Though the area has a sinister history which pre-dates Crowley's arrival. The house is said to be built on the grounds where a church once stood. Legend has it that it caught fire with the entire congregation trapped inside who subsequently perished.

Led Zeppelin guitarist Jimmy Page – a Crowley enthusiast purchased the property in 1970. Though he only spent six weeks at the house the entire time of his ownership. Leaving it in the hands of his friend and caretaker Malcolm Dent. Dent reported some very strange goings on whilst at the house. Including what sounded like a wild animal snorting and banging outside his room. Page sold the property in 1992. Occult experimental filmmaker Kenneth Anger – another Crowley devotee also rented the house for a while prior to Page's ownership in 1969.

Adjacent to the property across the road is Boleskine Cemetery which overlooks the loch. There was rumoured to be a tunnel leading from the house to the mortuary room in the corner of the cemetery grounds.

The last owners were a wealthy couple from the Netherlands who used the house as a holiday retreat. They'd been out shopping in Inverness just before Christmas of 2015 when they came home to find the house completely ablaze. The fire destroyed 60% of the house making it unliveable. The house sat lying dormant and half destroyed for the next few years, attracting all kinds of shady characters curious of it's dark history. It fell prey to another fire in July 2019. This time it was suspected arson, though no perpetrators to date have been apprehended.

Though just before the second fire the house was purchased by property developers Keith and Kyra Readdy. They in turn set up the Boleskine House Foundation and set out restoring the house in it's original incarnation brick by brick. A literal phoenix rising from the ashes. At the time of writing they have started self guided audio tours of work in progress which I recently attended. I'd visited the house twice before in 2011 and 2016 after the first fire.

They have a zero tolerance policy for uninvited trespassers.

Can't really blame them , they were plagued by an unwanted homeless man who kept showing up at the property unannounced and wouldn't leave. He was even banned by an Inverness Sheriff Court order from going within 8.7 miles of the house but still kept showing up! He was eventually arrested and given a jail sentence.

*

I caught up with Keith to get the low down on the Boleskine House Foundation and re- development.

Tell me about the Boleskine House Foundation . How many are on the team and what is the work schedule?

The Boleskine House Foundation is a registered charity in Scotland. Our objectives reach far and wide, but our primary reason for being established is to rebuild the B-listed eighteenth-century manor house Boleskine House and revitalize its estate for the benefit of the general public. Our other aims include education, recreation, and environmental sustainability. Our team runs exclusively on unpaid volunteer labour, with several people from around the world lending their skills and expertise to helping our organization operate. Our executive board consists of a board of trustees, four in number who see to the day to day decision-making for the charity.

Explain how and when you came into possession of the property. Did you have to dismantle the whole remains after the fires and start building from scratch?

At the time of the property coming on the market in 2019, we saw an opportunity to reinstate a previously neglected building into something that could benefit a greater community. The way we saw it, there is only one Boleskine House, and to have allowed the reamining house to be demolished or developed on the way it was being marketed would have been a horrible fate to a remarkable building. As property developers in England, we found the courage to take on the collosal project. Most everything was destroyed by the time we purchased the house except for the 12 foot high granite walls, which were also in bad shape from the two fires. To answer your question, we nearly started from scratch.

Where do you want to take this and what are the goals upon completion ? Do you plan on turning it into an exhibition or museum with an emphasis on the whole Aleister Crowley/Jimmy Page ownership?

Our first goal is to make it a lovely property again. We would like to see Boleskine become a educational, artistic, recreational and cultural hub unlike anything else in the UK, blending in its intriguing history in Scotland with the peculiar and fascinating subjects of esotericism and mysticism that surround its mystique, along with honouring its history in music and the arts.

Boleskine House under reconstruction. Photo courtesy of the Boleskine House Foundation.

*

The adjacent Boleskine Cemetery is also shrouded in it's own mystery . It is said to be a hotbed for paranormal activity attracting occult thrill seekers and Crowley aficionados on Halloween. Crowley themed graffiti has been repeatedly found in the ground's old mortuary room. In the late sixties there was talk of an active cult in the area who worshipped the ancient serpent goddess Tiamat.

In 1969, whilst exploring the cemetery a group of American students came across a piece of tapestry wrapped in a sea shell. It was around four by five feet and adorned with snake imagery. Though there was never any evidence of such a cult and this just adds to the many urban legends surrounding this place. The fact that this would have been around the exact time that occult filmmaker Kenneth Anger was renting the house answers the question of this particular incident right there.

Photo courtesy of the Boleskine House Foundation.

It's easy enough to get to , all you do is follow the B852 from Inverness which morphs into General Wade's Military Road. However if you don't have your own transport, buses are fairly limited. The 302 operates five services a day there and back on weekdays and Saturdays. Sundays there is no service provided. The bus trip takes around forty minutes and constantly has to give way for on coming traffic as the road is so narrow. There is no official bus stop outside the house but it is recognised as a stop so the driver will let you off and pick you up from there.

The creepy Boleskine Cemetery. A hotbed for paranormal and cult activity.

Guernsey Witchcraft and Pagan Folklore

As well as World War ll fortifications, Guernsey also as it's share of mystical places with interesting folkloric tales attached to them.

There are several megalithic dolmens each with their own story .

Le Trepied dolmen was built during the neolithic period – 400 – 2500 BC. It is on the seafront beside a gun batterie. It is said to have been the meeting place for the island's witches and wizards who met every Friday night for their sabbats. They were shapeshifters who took the form of animals and danced back to back. These sabbats were allegedly attended by the Devil who provided a feast of bread and wine for his followers.

La Varde Dolmen is located on L'Ancresse Common on the northern part of the island. One has to walk across a golf course to get access to it. It is a prehistoric passage grave with a length of ten metres. It is the largest surviving megalithic structure on Guernsey. The tomb was discovered during military exercises in 1811. Burnt and unburnt human bones and skulls were found on the site upon discovery. The entrance is low and one has to crouch down to gain access to the interior.

Le Trepied Dolmen.

Sign post at Le Trepied depicting the folklore tale
of the Devil's Sabbat.

La Varde entrance.

Interior of the La Varde tomb.

Looking out from the interior.

La Table des Pions – commonly known as the Fairy Ring is located at the south-western point of Pleinmont headland. It consists of a dug out circular ditch with a circle of stones lying around the outside. Construction of the site is unknown but it is thought to have been in the late 18th or 19th century. It's true purpose is also unknown though it is thought to have religious pagan origins. Some say that it was constructed as a picnic area for highland officials who inspected roads and coastal defences.

Of course there are many folkloric tales surrounding this site, including a meeting spot for fairies and witches. It is located at somewhat of a magical location right on the seafront. To get there you have to make your way to the Imperial Hotel. From there is a road which takes you right to the site . It is around a twenty minute walk but it is very pleasant as it is right on the seafront and witnessing the crashing waves on the right day is a site to behold. You also pass a WW2 German bunker and a fortress that was built in 1680 Fort Pezeries. The Germans used it as a machine gun post during the occupation. The Fairy Ring is directly opposite the fort.

The only downside on my visit was the perimeter was fenced off. It wasn't a hindrance but would have looked better without the fence for photo purposes.

German WW2 bunker on the walk
to the Fairy Ring.

The author in front of Fort Pezeries.

Le Dehus Dolmen is located in the northern part of Guernsey. Unlike the other dolmens on the island it is a fully enclosed chamber. There is a gate which opens to a door which one has to crouch down to gain entrance. There is also a light switch on the left of the entrance which lights up the whole inner chamber. It is approximately ten metres in length, the entrance is narrow and low but once inside it is quite spacious with plenty of standing room. There is also two smaller chambers either side of the passage. The inner chamber features a central standing stone with a carved bearded face and a series of symbolic designs.

Tower Hill Steps in the centre of St Peter Port in Guernsey bares a memorial plaque that reflects the barbarity of early Christianity. In 1556 three women – Katherine Cawches, Guillemine Gilbert and Perotine Massey (along with her unborn child) were tried as heretics for their protestant faith and burnt at the stake. The plaque is on the right hand side halfway up the steps.

The low door entrance to Le Dehus Dolmen.

Opposite page: La Table des Pions –
The Fairy Ring.

Le Delus inner chamber.

One of the smaller chambers
on the side of the passage.

Tower Hill Steps , St Peter Port Guernsey.

To the memory of

Katherine Cawches
Guillemine Gilbert
Perotine Massey

All believers in the Lord Jesus Christ,
who on, or about, 18th July 1556,
and near this site, were cruelly
burned to death at the stake
for their Protestant faith.
The latter named was pregnant at
the time of martyrdom and
gave birth to a son in the flames.
The child was retrieved, but it
was ordered that he be thrown back.

Faithful unto death.................Rev 2:10

Memorial plaque for the victims of Christian persecution.

Channel Islands Nazi Occupation

During the second world war the British dependent Channel Islands in the English Channel off the coast of Normandy, France were under military occupation by Nazi Germany. The occupation lasted from June 30, 1940 until May 9, 1945 – Liberation Day.

After the allied defeat at the Battle of France the British Government decided that the Channel Islands were of no strategic importance and would therefore not be defended. The islands served no strategic purpose to the Germans either, other than the propaganda value of having occupied British territory. It was also one step away from occupying Britain itself.

Using mainly slave labour the German forces along with civil and military engineering Organisation Todt set about fortifying the islands, Hitler wanted to transform the islands into an impregnable fortress. Constructing bunkers, tunnels, gun emplacements, air raid shelters and other concrete fortifications as part of his Atlantic Wall. The life expectancy of the slave workers was around two weeks. The Germans figured it would be cheaper to work and starve them to death and simply replace them rather than adequately feed them.

I spent two years in the Channel Islands visiting such places. I've spent time on all the islands with the exception of Jersey. Most of these fortifications still stand today. Some of them very well maintained with regular upkeep. Driving around Guernsey in particular, you can't help but notice the sheer amount of bunkers at the side of roads and in grass embankments. The place is littered with them. Some are left lying dormant, dilapidated and in a state of disrepair covered in graffiti. Others are owned by museums and undergo regular restoration for tourism, even containing mannequins dressed in WW2 uniforms at machine gun posts.

The first place I visited was the L shaped MP4 L'Angle Observation Tower overlooking the sea cliffs on the south -western tip of the island. One is free to enter and explore the interior. It has three floors but is derelict and unsafe. You have to be very careful where you put your footing so do so at your own risk. Also in the vicinity across the field and up a steep slope of steps is the impressive Batterie Dollman, with a renovated gun platform and large artillery piece which gets fired on the Liberation Day holiday.

There is also a series of tunnels, bunkers, shelters and munition rooms connected to the emplacement. From the ground level they are totally hidden by the dense undergrowth. Upon first observation you wouldn't even know they were there. One has to venture into the dense shrubs to gain access to the ancillary trenches, but it really is a fascinating place to explore.

Around a kilometre up the road is the five story MP3 Naval Observation Tower. It is comprised of 2 metre thick concrete and visually impressive. However it is owned by the Occupation Museum and has very limited opening times – Wednesday and Sunday 2-4.30pm.

MP4 L'Angle Observation Tower
overlooking the sea cliffs.

Battery Dollman gun emplacement.
The gun gets fired every Liberation Day holiday on May 9.

Ancillary trenches hidden under the undergrowth leading to the gun platform.

MP3 five story naval observation tower in Pleinmont , Guernsey.

Guernsey also hosts two impressive military museums. There is the La Valette. Located on the waterfront in St Peter Port it is a set of complex tunnels dug into the side of a hill which the Germans used as a fuel storage facility for their U Boats.

The other is the German Occupation Museum located close to the Guernsey Airport. This is owned and operated by long time collector Richard Heaume and features an authentic recreation of an occupation era street. Both museums have an extensive collection of authentic WW2 artifacts and are an absolute must for any WW2 enthusiast.

Entrance to La Valette Military Museum.

Display case at
La Valette Museum.

The German Occupation Museum.

By far one of the most bleakest places I've visited is the German Underground Hospital and Ammunition Store. Located in St Andrew in the centre of Guernsey it is the largest remaining World War 2 structure in the Channel Islands. Covering 75,000 square feet it is a vast maze of underground tunnels built under a low hill.

25, 823 cubic metres of rock were excavated and 9,053 cubic metres of concrete were poured for it's construction.

As bleak as it is, visiting the place is a fascinating experience. It is cold, damp and cloaked with a deathlike silence with not an ounce of daylight. The only sound being the echo of one's footsteps. It has a genuinely creepy atmosphere and you certainly wouldn't want to spend a night here.

Although it is somewhat of an underground labyrinth it is well sign posted and easy to make your way around. Some of the features include – hospital wards with beds, operating theatre, mortuary, kitchen, store rooms, cinema and weapons and equipment exhibition. There are also information boards on the construction of the hospital and some of the slave workers who built it.

The place does have a grim atmosphere but it is still an interesting visit and highly recommended. It is an experience you will not forget.

Opening times may vary depending on time of season so it's always a good idea to check their website first before planning your visit.

Opposite page: The dark atmospheric tunnels
of the underground hospital.

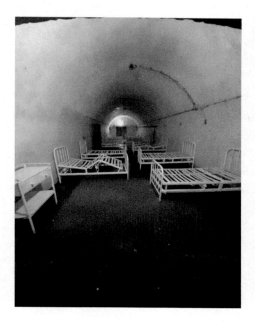

Hospital ward.

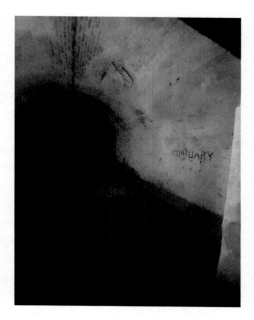

Mortuary.

Ward.

Festung Guernsey is a voluntary incentive devoted to the excavation, restoration and preservation of these historical sites and fortifications. I caught up with the group whilst visiting Batteries Mirus and Scharnhorst.

Paul Bourgaize outlined the group's initiative:

The demise of the former Tourist Board and Heritage Committee joint "Fortress Guernsey" programme in 2003 caused widespread consternation and disappointment.

With awareness and interest in the Atlantic Wall fortifications continuing to grow, the shortsighted and premature abandonment of the States' initiative was deeply felt by local restorers and operators of the German sites.

Following a successful meeting of interested parties in October 2005, a decision was reached to launch a similar initiative named Festung Guernsey, aiming to:

- Promote interest in local German fortifications, nationally and internationally.

- Promote the island as a destination for special interest holidays.

- Bring all interested site owners and operators together to promote existing sites under one entity.

- Provide information for potential visitors.

- Identify examples of significant bunker types not currently preserved, and secure selective examples for long-term conservation and make them available for inspection by interested parties.

To this end the project has gone from strength to strength. We now have a large group of volunteers of all ages, with a range of skills working regularly on a number of sites. Much of the group's work is of a practical nature involving many hours digging, renovating and landscaping various sites. Artefacts are carefully restored and re-used were possible or put into storage for future use.

We have secured leases on a number of sites and have also worked with both the Environment and Culture & Leisure Departments to excavate fortifications at Vale Castle, Le Guet and Fort Hommet. We've worked closely with the probation service providing tasks for offenders given community service orders. At the time of writing we're responsible for 24 bunkers across 10 sites.

We work with a number of tour guides who provide tours of our sites, and also work with several European specialist tour operators providing military tours. All work is voluntary and as a non-profit making organisation we rely mostly on donations and book sales to fund the various projects.

Research is also an important part of our work, with many of the batteries, resistance nests and strong points around the island needing investigation. Maps are produced and the structures measured and drawn up. We are now the first port of call for States Departments and private landowners seeking information on bunkers on their land, and we can provide advice on restoration and excavation .

Considerable time is also spent on research in the U.K. and Europe. The group has a growing archive of plans and photographs relating to the 1940's period

Many supporters have professional qualifications that assist in the running of our projects. The diverse membership also networks throughout the community, smoothing the way for current and future projects. A great deal of work is carried out by individuals specialising in their own particular fields of interest.

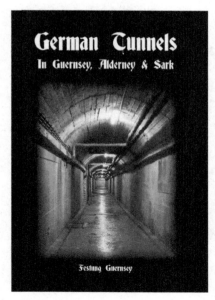

Self published book on German Tunnels on
Guernsey, Alderney and Sark.

Batteries Scharnhorst and Mirus are located on the west coast of Guernsey. They are on private land however tours can be booked through Tours of Guernsey. I will stress however that these tours only operate in the seasonal months. Both locations are surrounded by fields and during the winter months they are inaccessible with vehicles as the land becomes very marshy with the rain. If you can get a tour in before the season ends though it is definitely worth it. They are comprised of trenches, bunkers, ammunition rooms and gun emplacements. Mirus is the largest gun batterie in the Channel Islands and features authentic Nazi insignia on the walls.

Trenches at Batterie Scharnhorst.

Signage on an ammunition room
at Scharnhorst.

Entrance to bunkers at
Batterie Mirus

Authentic Nazi eagle insignia adorns a bunker
wall at Mirus.

Alderney, the northernmost of the Channel Islands also has it's share of German World War ll bunkers and fortifications. Indeed it was host to the only four concentration camps on British soil. Including the notorious SS run Lager Sylt.

I visited the island in January 2023, it is only a ten minute flight from Guernsey via a Dornier 228NG nineteen passenger light aircraft. It took me two days to get there due to cancellation of flights because of bad weather. Alderney Airport is by far the tiniest I've visited. Its terminal is only a small low level building which houses arrivals/departures and the café. They don't even have a luggage scanning machine, it is done manually!

I called a taxi and decided my first port of call would be the SS Lager Sylt grounds. As it's practically on the airport grounds at the rear.

The only thing that remains of the camp are three gateposts with a memorial plaque mounted on the second from right. There is also an old water trough and what look like concrete sentry posts below the undergrowth. Other than that there is only a disused air navigation building which was built as a part of the airport long after the camp was abandoned. It's hard to imagine the atrocities which took place here. Around 400 people lost their lives at Lager Sylt.

The driver informed me that the owner of the taxi company, Bill – funny enough named 'Bill's Taxis' offered detailed tours of the island for an affordable fee. So, he dropped me at my accommodation and I took one of his cards. The following day's activities sorted.

THESE GATE POSTS MARK
THE ENTRANCE TO THE FORMER
GERMAN CONCENTRATION CAMP
"S.S. LAGER · SYLT"
SOME 400 PRISONERS DIED HERE
BETWEEN
MARCH 1943 AND JUNE 1944
THIS PLAQUE WAS PLACED BY
EX-PRISONERS AND THEIR FAMILIES
2008

Opposite page: SS Lager Sylt Concentration Camp gateposts. The only thing left to indicate it was ever there.

Water trough on camp grounds.

THESE GATE POSTS MARK
THE ENTRANCE TO THE FORMER
GERMAN CONCENTRATION CAMP
"S.S. LAGER - SYLT"
SOME 400 PRISONERS DIED HERE
BETWEEN
MARCH 1943 AND JUNE 1944
THIS PLAQUE WAS PLACED BY
EX PRISONERS AND THEIR FAMILIES
2008

Memorial plaque mounted on Sylt gatepost.

Bill picked me up from my hotel and we began the tour. He is a former sergeant in the British army and is very knowledgeable on the island and its history, particularly the Nazi occupation years. The tour lasted for two hours and for £40 it was well worth it. We started off at the bunkers at Braye Bay followed by The Odeon, a massive four floor concrete tower that was used for naval findings. It is well preserved containing detailed information boards and mannequins dressed in uniforms operating equipment.

We then made our way to the Nunnery Roman Fort which has well preserved sign posted WW2 bunkers. Along the way Bill filled me in on other interesting historic sights of Alderney including a mass ancient burial site. The previous driver had indicated that Alderney sometimes had a strange energy about it. The inexplainable feeling of being watched.

It is however a beautiful place, and not just for WW2 history buffs. The main town St Anne is sparsely populated with some pleasant bars, cafes and restaurants. It's almost like going back in time seeing business' on the main street close for a few hours in the afternoon to reopen later. It has a real peaceful laid back feel to it. You barely see anyone in the streets.

Alderney also hosts the only working railway in the Channel Islands. Two old London Underground carriages towed by a diesel engine on a scenic coastal route from Braye Bay to Mannez Quarry and Lighthouse. Unfortunately it was under repair on my visit therefore not operating.

I intend on spending longer than my mere three day stay on my next visit.

Opposite page: German bunkers overlooking Braye Bay, Alderney.

The Odeon naval finding
MP3 concrete tower.

German bunker at The Nunnery Roman
Fort, Alderney.

There are many more photos I could have included within this chapter. However due to space and the length of this book I had to be somewhat selective. Though it's gotta be said that the Channel Islands Occupation could easily be a full photographic book within itself. There is just so much to see and cover. As mentioned earlier in this chapter Jersey has many of these structures which I am yet to see. I fully intend on remedying that.

Abbey Of Thelema

In 1920 British occult mystic Aleister Crowley along with his assistant and mistress Leah Hirsig (The Scarlet Woman) set out to form a spiritual and magical school based on the teachings of Crowley's religion Thelema. This spiritual centre was in the form of a villa in the small fishing town of Cefalu in Northern Sicily. It was to be an idealistic utopia whereupon the inhabitants were encouraged to live by their own free will and pursue their inner pleasures. This was to be known as the Abbey Of Thelema.

Regular activities included the daily worship of the sun, studies of Crowley's writings and other ritual practises as well as general domestic chores.

However this ideal commune proved to be short lived. In 1923 one of Crowley's devotees Raoul Loveday succumbed to a typhoid fever and died at the Abbey. Loveday's wife Betty May blamed his death on the participation in one of Crowley's rituals, allegedly consuming the blood of a sacrificed cat. However there was no evidence to support this and in reality Loveday's death was probably as a result of drinking unsafe water from a mountain spring, something which Crowley had warned them both against.

Nevertheless, May returned To London and gave a nefarious account to the tabloids of all the debaucherous goings on at the Abbey, overseen by who the British press referred to as 'The Wickedest Man In the World'..

Of course stories of wild drug consumption and satanic orgies also got back to the then Italian fascist government of Benito Mussolini and Crowley and his followers were promptly ordered to leave country.

The villa was abandoned after that, with locals whitewashing over Crowley's murals on the walls. To this day, locals consider it cursed ground and don't go near the place. However over the years it's become a place of pilgrimage for Crowley enthusiasts the world over, including filmmaker Kenneth Anger who uncovered and filmed some of the murals for his lost film *Thelema Abbey* (1955).

It is now a dilapidated ruin with all the original murals faded beyond recognition and no longer visible. It is of course covered in graffiti from recent visits of Crowley enthusiasts. I visited there in 2019 and have to say if you plan on visiting, then do so at your own risk. Firstly it's officially off limits and considered trespass to enter. There are warning signs against entry, there is also a wire fence around the perimeter but someone had cut a hole in the fence using wire cutters. That's how I got in , of course I took this risk. This place was on my list for years so how could I not?

You also have to be careful where you put your footing as the track leading down to the abbey is dangerously overgrown and unstable. There are also spikey thorns from tree branches. However if you are game to make the pilgrimage firstly you have to take a flight to the Sicilian capital Palermo. From there you take the train to Cefalu which takes around 50mins. It is quite a pleasant journey as you get some awesome views of the northern Sicilian coastline. Cefalu is a small town but finding a taxi at the station upon arrival is not difficult. I'd advise booking accommodation in advance. I stayed at the B&B Roomantic which is the closest property to the Abbey. Seriously, it's virtually in the backyard. I arrived checked in, and the walk to the abbey was just around the corner. It's very easy to find. Look for the Stadio Comunale Football Stadium and it's directly opposite on a narrow street. The dilapidated roof is clearly visible.

The Abbey's ruins clearly visible from the narrow street opposite the football stadium.

Once you make your way down to the front of the house the only entrance is the only open window which isn't boarded up. This was also Crowley's bedroom - La Chambre Des Cauchemars – The Room of Nightmares. There is a small ledge below the window arch to stand on, you lever yourself up and in you go. The dark green pealing paintwork is instantly recognisable. The original murals are long gone and the walls are covered with graffiti and drawings from visiting Crowley aficionados . But one can't help but think – if only these walls could talk.

La Chambre des Cauchemars – The Room of Nightmares. Crowley's bedroom.

From there you make your way through the doorway to an adjacent room containing bunk bed frames which look like they could have been there since the Great Beast's departure in 1923, but who knows. Highly unlikely. This leads you out into what used to be the living room, kitchen and bathroom. The floor is overgrown with weeds and covered in debris. It's also open air with the massive hole in the roof.

I explored the remains of the Abbey for around an hour before returning to the B&B. I had a very pleasant experience at the Roomantic. The host Louisa is an American who has lived in Sicily for over thirty years. She was a lovely lady and very hospitable. My room had a balcony with an awesome view overlooking the Med.

Of course there are other things to do in Cefalu. The town has some fantastic cafes and restaurants. There's the 12th century Norman cathedral with it's twin towers. One can take a hike to the summit of the rock with a spectacular view overlooking the town and the ocean. There's also ruins of a Norman castle on the summit. A walk on the beach front is an impressive activity. It still looks like the ancient sea port and has a very Lovecraftian feel to it. I fully intend to plan another visit at some stage.

Aleister Crowley in full ceremonial garb during his time in occult group The Golden Dawn.

The sigil of Thelema Aleister Crowley's religion.

Above – the Lovecraftian looking seafront of Cefalu.

The view from my balcony.

Sunset in Cefalu.

Ehrenhalle / Luitpold Arena

I did cover Nuremberg's Nazi Party Rally Grounds in the first edition of this book. However there was one location I missed which has considerable historical significance. The Ehrenhalle (hall of honour) and the former Luitpold Arena. Located directly across the road from the Dokumentationzentrum (Documentation Centre). I paid a second visit to the grounds in 2019 to see what I'd missed first time round. In 1934 the Nazi Party held the Totenehrung (honouring of the dead) ceremony for the German soldiers killed in World War I and the 16 killed in Hitler's failed 1923 putsch to seize power in Munich.

Adolf Hitler, SS leader Heinrich Himmler and SA leader Viktor Lutze marched 240 metres down the broad marble road from the Luitpold Tribune to the front of the Ehrenhalle where they gave the Nazi salute. 150,000 other participants filled the arena. It was a very symbolic ceremony and a gesture of Nazi strength, unity and triumph.

Luitpold Arena was initially Luitpold Grove and was named after Bavarian ruler. Hitler had the crescent shaped tribune built along with the marble road leading to Ehrenhalle. The Tribune was designed to accommodate 50,000 spectators. Of course like the other rally grounds remnants the glory days of the past are long gone. The only thing that remains intact in it's original form is the arcaded Ehrenhalle itself. Along with the adjacent cobbled stone terrace with five pillars either side that were used for fire bowls. They have not been ignited since the last rally held here in 1938. The engraved text as been upgraded to honour the those killed in World War ll and under the Nazi regime. A war memorial adorned with an eagle stands at the back of Ehrenhalle but the rest of it is just a vast green parkland with trees. All the other buildings were demolished. It is also restored to it's original name Luitpold Grove. Parts of the original granite staircases can be seen and there is information panels all around the park as a reminder of it's history. Getting there from central Nuremberg is simple enough. A tram or number 36 bus takes you straight there and takes around eight minutes.

Above – Parts of the original granite staircase can be seen as well as historical information panels.

Below – A war memorial behind Ehrenhalle.

The former Nazi rally ground is now a picturesque parkland . Though one can make out the imprint of the marble road where the Nazi leaders strode once was .

The author beside the memorial statue for the victims of the disaster.

Chernobyl

With the current war in Ukraine still going on with no end in sight at the time of writing, all trips to the Chernobyl Exclusion Zone are currently cancelled indefinitely. I was lucky enough to visit there in 2019 when the current situation was unthinkable.

The Chernobyl Nuclear Reactor disaster occurred on April 26 1986 when RBMK Reactor 4 exploded whilst a negligent safety test was being conducted running the reactor at dangerously low power. Designer flaws in the reactor also contributed to the accident. The reactor's core exploded releasing huge amounts of radiation into the atmosphere, spreading to Russia, Belarus, other parts of Europe and Scandinavia. The residents in the neighbouring city of Pripyat were evacuated never to return. Several plant workers and firefighters lost their lives as a result of radiation poisoning. It was the worst nuclear disaster in history to date. Attempts were made by the then communist government of the Soviet Union but NASA picked it up and it wasn't long before the whole world knew what went down.

The events of the disaster have been covered by countless documentaries in years gone by as well as an HBO miniseries.

Tours to the plant began in 2011 when tourist interest grew and scientists realized the radiation levels were diminishing.

Gamma Travel based in Kiev are the tour operators when they are operating. On this occasion I chose an eight hour tour which included a visit to the plant, a former top secret Soviet military base and Pripyat. The tour started outside the Dnipro Hotel just around the corner from Maidan Square in central Kiev. We stopped for a bite to eat at a service station before continuing our journey to the Exclusion Zone which is a two hour drive north of Kiev. There were two guides , the driver the tour guide herself Maria, a pretty girl with flouro pink hair who spoke perfect fluent English and was very knowledgeable on the area and subject. At the entrance to the Exclusion Zone we were subject to security checks whereupon Maria had to show all the relevant paperwork to entrance security officials. We were free to leave the bus and stretch our legs so I took it upon myself to check out some of the crazy merchandise stands and purchased some fridge magnets.

The merch stand at the Exclusion Zone Entrance. They sold everything from t-shirts to glow in the dark condoms!

The first stop was the former top secret Soviet Duga 1 Radar Base. It was so secret that it wasn't even on the map during it's operation in the Cold War. It was marked on the map as a 'summer camp' and is hidden in the forest of northern Ukraine.

The radar itself is a gigantic imposing steel structure. 450ft in height and 2,300ft in length. It was built in the 1950's as a over the horizon early warning missile defence system. It's intimidating just looking at it.

The imposing Duga 1 radar system. A product of the Soviet era Cold War.

Next stop was the abandoned Kopachi Village which featured a kindergarten, the only remaining building along with a war memorial. All the other wooden buildings were demolished and buried in the ground after the disaster. A haunting eerie calm hung in the air. Maria had her Geiger Counter and showed us a couple of radioactive hot spots. It was then on to the power plant where it all happened on that fateful night of April 26, 1986.

As we approached the plant we pulled over to get some panoramic shots of the cooling towers and the gigantic arch-shaped steel structure which now confines where reactor 4 once stood as well as the makeshift sarcophagus which was hastily constructed after the disaster. From there it was on to the Chernobyl Plant canteen for a Soviet era Cold War lunch which was included in the price of the tour. We were checked for radiation via a body scan upon arrival and when we left.

Distant panoramic shot of the plant with cooling towers and canal.

Close up shot of the plant with its arch-shaped steel structure.

The author at the welcome to the city of Chernobyl sign.

The meal at the canteen consisted of chicken schnitzel and rice, a salad with salami, a bowl of vegetable soup, bread and a glass of orange cordial. I wouldn't have been happy if I'd have paid for this at a café or restaurant. It was average at best and reminded me of the lunches served up at the school canteen when I was a kid. But this was the Chernobyl canteen and I wanted something authentic that would have been served up in the Soviet era Cold War so I was happy . From there it was back to the bus and on to Pripyat.

Cold War style lunch in the plant canteen consisting of chicken schnitzel, rice, salad, soup and bread.

Pripyat is only a ten minute drive from the power plant. We disembarked from the bus and began our two hour of the former city on foot. It totally lived up to everything I'd seen and read about it. An apocalyptic ghost of a city that has been ravaged by time and nature. The place has an eerie silence about it with all the decaying dilapidated buildings slowly being swallowed up by the surrounding forest. A once thriving Soviet dream city of the future being claimed back by nature.

The first port of call was the landmark amusement park with the ferris wheel and dodgem cars. It's interesting to note that these attractions were never used. They were set up for a May Day Festival just before the disaster.

The landmark ferris wheel of Pripyat.

From there we made our way to an abandoned supermarket. This was the first of it's kind in the Soviet Union when Pripyat was built in the 70's. Up until then people did their grocery shopping at small stores manned by one person. Often waiting in long queues.

Maria showed us another hot spot with her Geiger counter. Next up was the Polissya Hotel , one of the tallest buildings in Pripyat. It was built to house delegations and guests visiting the power plant. Maria said it was built much bigger than needed to give off a good impression to the visitors.

It was then on to the dilapidated entertainment centre which housed a concert hall and a cinema. And we really had to be careful here as it was pitch dark and there were missing floorboards. The cinema seats were partially intact.

Radiation hot spot.

Most of the high rise apartment windows were smashed. This is of course caused by disrepair but was also a result of the occupants attempting to save their furniture and belongings upon evacuation. Though they were limited to what they could take on the evacuation buses. Most of them didn't mind as they were told they would be returning.

We then made our way to the school. Communist era portraits of politicians were stacked up the corner of one of the rooms. One of the classrooms was also littered with gas masks. Next up was the landmark empty Azure swimming pool. It actually remained in use until 1998, twelve years after the disaster. It was mainly used by Chernobyl liquidators in that time.

Polissya Hotel.

Our final port of call was the Pripyat River. Where a radioactive barge was lying dormant. One area that was strictly off limits was the hospital. This is because the firefighters clothing from the disaster is stored in the basement and is still highly radioactive.

It was then back on the bus for the two hour journey back to Kiev. We were body scanned for radiation upon leaving the Exclusion Zone. It was a memorable tour which I'd love to do again when the war is over and things return to normal and the tours resume.

I did this tour in November so the weather was just right. Summers can be hot and winters are freezing with snow on the ground.

There is a two day tour which Gamma Travel offer whereupon they put you up in a hotel in the city of Chernobyl. Think I'll do that one next time. Definitely worth it.

Azure abandoned swimming pool.　　　Radioactive barge on Pripyat River.

Bumper car park and abandoned apartment block in Pripyat.

112 Ocean Avenue , Amityville , Long Island

Well this three story Dutch colonial five bedroom house certainly needs no introductions. It spawned a best selling book in 1977 followed by the movie in 1979 and has since been followed by sixteen sequels and a remake.Though only the first three were inspired by the 'true events' that took place, all the rest were mainly straight-to-video releases associated by name and imagery only. With it's sinister Jack 'O Lantern style windows, it has become somewhat iconic and one of the most recognised houses in the world. Though upon visiting it in it's suburban tranquility, it's hard to imagine what took place here.

The events of the Amityville Horror began on November 13, 1974 when Ronald 'Butch' DeFeo Jr murdered his entire family whilst they slept with .35 Calibre Lever Action Marlin 336c rifle. He received six life sentences and died in prison on March 12 , 2021 aged 69.

The property remained empty for thirteen months until George and Kathy Lutz moved in with their three children in December 1975. The Lutz family were only there for 28 days before fleeing in terror leaving behind all their furniture and belongings claiming to be terrorised by paranormal forces. A story they stuck with until their deaths. The case was subject to massive media attention and paranormal investigations. Namely from celebrity couple Ed and Lorraine Warren, self proclaimed psychic mediums, clairvoyants and demonologists. Of course, there has been much criticism over the years of the truthfulness of the case, with many sceptics claiming it to be an elaborate hoax citing many inconsistences in the Lutz's story. Also no owners since the Lutz's have reported any strange goings on. However, there are an equal amount of believers who regard their story as totally credible. Whatever the case, the story has certainly cemented it's place in history. I for one have had pretty much a lifelong interest in it which compelled me to visit in 2022.

To get there from New York City, you need to catch a Babylon bound train on the Long Island Rail Road from Pennsylvania Station. Amityville is around an hour's journey on that line. Once you get off, walk down Broadway until you come to Merrick Road. High Fedility record store is directly across the street. From there, you cross and go left until you come to Ocean Avenue. You walk around two blocks and you can't miss it. Gone are the sinister Jack 'O Lantern windows, but it's still instantly recognisable. Though remember it's privately owned, so respect the residents privacy and don't go trespassing, there is nothing to stop you photographing the house from the road. You can also view the rear of the house with the boathouse from Riverside Avenue on the other side. You just walk back down Ocean Avenue cross the bridge over Amityville Creek and turn right. It's only a narrow channel as opposed to the big river depicted in the movie, though that was filmed on an entirely different location in Toms River, New Jersey.

The front of the house on Ocean Avenue.

The rear of the house with the boathouse on
Riverside Avenue overlooking Amityville Creek.

The sinister face of the Amityville Horror House
on patches. From the author's collection.

Cecil Hotel

Of course whilst in Los Angeles I just had to pay a visit to it's most infamous landmark. The Cecil Hotel is a fourteen floor building with 700 guest rooms. It is located at 640 S Main Street in downtown Los Angeles, just one block from the city's notorious Skid Row. It was opened on December 20, 1924 as a budget hotel.

Over the years it developed a reputation for violence, suicides and overdoses. Attracting drug dealers, junkies, prostitutes and even serial killers, most notably Night Stalker Richard Ramirez.

In 2021 it was the subject of a Netflix documentary series *The Vanishing At Cecil Hotel*. The series covered the case of 21 year old Canadian student Elissa Lam who went missing whilst staying at the hotel. She was last seen alive on CCTV footage acting erratically in the hotel elevator repeatedly pressing buttons appearing to be hiding from someone. Her nude body was discovered in the water tank on the hotel roof after residents complained of the pressure, colour and taste of the water. Foul play was ruled out as it was discovered she suffered from severe bipolar and was prone to strange erratic behaviour when she didn't take her medication. It was concluded that she climbed into the tank herself whilst suffering a breakdown.

Many former residents and employees claim the place is consumed by a dark energy. Some even describing it as a portal to hell. Bad things just kept happening on a regular basis.

The Cecil also inspired the *American Horror Story: Hotel* season. I visited the hotel in January 2021. It is now an affordable housing complex operated by Skid Row Housing Trust and closed to the public. I took a cab there from West Hollywood and stopped just to grab a couple of photos and have a brief chat with the security guard at the front entrance which is now a side door for residents next to the former entrance to the hotel lobby.

It would have been cool to have known someone who could have got me in there. Just to explore where all this shit happened, particularly Richard Ramirez's old room. I grabbed my photos and was back in the cab outta there. I didn't want to be hanging around near Skid Row which can be a dangerous, unpredictable place. So it was on to Lemmy's Lounge at the Rainbow in West Hollywood. The amount of homeless people in Los Angeles is incredible. They can be seen everywhere in makeshift tents, even under freeway bridges. And 'Tinsel Town' is no exception.

Whilst in LA, I also visited the house at 8763 Wonderland Avenue, Laurel Canyon, location of what is known as the 'Wonderland Murders'. In July 1981, four members of the notorious drug dealing 'Wonderland Gang' were found bludgeoned to death in the three story house. A brutal act of retribution allegedly masterminded by LA drug dealer and nightclub owner Eddie Nash. He was robbed in a home invasion by the gang two days earlier. 70's porn star John Holmes - an associate of the gang - was also implicated in the murders. I couldn't believe there was someone residing in the house where such a thing took place. Even though it happened a long time ago, the negative energy would still be rife. This event also inspired a 1990s movie, *Wonderland*, starring Val Kilmer as John Holmes and Eric Bogosian as Eddie Nash.

Whilst in LA, I also wanted to check out some of Charles Manson's former stomping grounds – Spahn Ranch and where the Tate/Polanski house once stood on Cielo Drive. But Scott Michaels, who ran Dearly Departed Tours, - exploring the locations of the dark side of Hollywood – no longer operates. Covid killed it stone dead.

The notorious Cecil Hotel, now an affordable housing complex closed to the public.
The iconic signage at the top of the building as reportedly been whitewashed over.

The Last Bookstore located near the Cecil, as featured in the Netflix documentary series. Elisa Lam did some shopping there before she went missing.

The author at the Wonderland Avenue house, location of the brutal Wonderland Murders.

Former Cecil Hotel lobby entrance.

Statue of iconic
Motorhead frontman
Lemmy at the Rainbow
Bar and Grill in West
Hollywood.
It was his second home
when he wasn't on tour.
I visited there after the
Cecil.

About the Author

Marquis is a self taught independent writer specializing in the dark and esoteric. Some of his previous titles include: *Devil's Disciples – Secret Societies, Historical Tyrants, Cults, Killers and Practitioners of the Black Arts, Letters From the Night Stalker – A Decade's Correspondence with Richard Ramirez, Faces of Horror – A Lifetime of Inspiration and Everlasting Impact.*

Eerie Planet – Second Edition is his seventh book and second guide to dark tourism. He has previously co-edited esoteric lifestyle magazine *The Sentinel* and creator of *Slices of Sin* Erotic Comic Book. He has been featured in various forms of the media including TV, magazines, newspapers and podcasts discussing Satanism and the Black Arts. He also an avid collector of horror movie merch, books, and travel souvenirs. His other passions include extreme music and exploring. He is currently based in the United Kingdom.

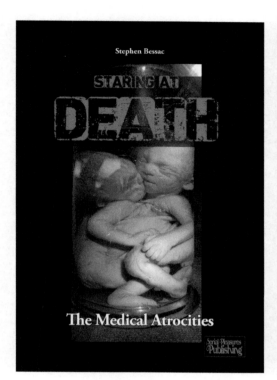

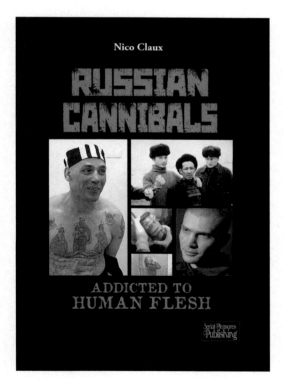

Printed in Great Britain
by Amazon

32139810R00084